Arabilis

Sundress Publications • Knoxville, TN

Editor: Marci Calabretta Cancio-Bello
Editorial Assistants: Anna Black

Special thanks to Stephanie Marker and Annie McIntosh.

Colophon: This book is set in Garamond.

Cover Design: Kristen Ton

Cover Art: "To Nurture" by Janelia Mould

Book Design: Danielle Alexander

Arabilis

Leah Silvieus

Acknowledgments

Many thanks to the generous editors of those magazines in which several of these poems first appeared, sometimes in different forms: AAWW's *The Margins*: "So Blonde;" *Anomaly*: "Elegy for Daylight" and "Matthew 19:14;" *Boxcar Poetry Review*: "Water Street Elegy;" *CURA*: "Nocturne with Seven Isles;" *diode*: "After Easter" and "On the Feast of Epiphany;" *Four Way Review*: "Epithalamium with Spider and Sparrow," "Hallasan," "Prayer to Saint Martha," and "Still Life with Fallen Game;" *Hyphen* magazine: "Field Elegy;" *Melusine*: "Equinox;" *NECK*: "Sonnet in Cold Blood;" *The Offing* (and to Nabila Lovelace): "Aubade at Low Tide;" *storySouth*: "The World Just Now, Emerging;" *A River & Sound Review*: for which "Nocturne with Volcanoes and Honey" was selected by Traci Brimhall for the Duckabush Prize for Poetry; *wildness*: "When Asked Where I'm (Really) From;" and *Washington Square Review* (and especially Jessica Marion Modi): "Aubade with Septic Field." Thanks also to Hyacinth Girl Press, who so generously and attentively ushered some of these poems into the world as a chapbook, *Anemochory*. Additional thanks to the Bull City Press team, including Ross White and Noah Stetzer for their work on *Season of Dares*, in which some of these poems have appeared—and all the love and gratitude to Leslie Sainz for her wisdom, her guidance, and the title for this collection.

Contents

Invocation

SUMMER

FALL

WINTER

SPRING

Benediction

For Sean

arabilis

ărābĭlis , e, adj. aro,

I. that can be ploughed, arable: "campus nullis arabilis tauris," Plin. 17, 5, 3, § 41.

— Charleton T. Lewis and Charles Short, *A Latin Dictionary*

O spirit
of difficult hunger
of sandstone
gunpowder
and Bud Light empties
of mud and grave
unmarked
bone   and fury
forget us not
we dirt-road
orphans   come
mercy-wild
come   asking
for a song

SUMMER

Matthew 19:14

after Jericho Brown
for the camp girls

Heaven belongs to such as these
      Your apostle taught us,

so Lord, let me not forget:
      those six girlhood summers down

that two-lane highway, left— past
      the seven-foot plastic Hereford bull

at Clearwater Junction; sleeping
      in cast-off army tents

where forty-miles-away
      might've been a different country, those

faraway towns' names exotic:
      Philipsburg, Frenchtown,

Wisdom, Choteau—
      bless those mouths red

with Fla-Vor-Ice, singing
      rise and shine and give God the glory,

glory. As we waited for the mess tent dinner bell
      the counselors decreed,

the last shall be first
      and the first shall be last

and we all turned 'round in line
        because we believed

that one day it'd be true.
        Lord forget us not in our hour

of need— those who dug Dixie cups
        from trash bins to tear into visions

of the Blessed Virgin, who stole change from Right to Life
        coin banks to buy Ring Pops for our little sisters.

Bless us, Lord, we dirt-road orphans, grown now
        and miles from the closest home—

girls once named for virtues
        our mothers hoped we'd hold true:

Faith, Joy, and daughter after daughter
                called Mercy.

Elegy for Daylight

Midsummer's 10 o'clock dusk had us
ditching swings, twisty slide 'n jungle
gym for the beyond. Boneyard. Field. Forest.
The mountain ash's galaxy of orange berries
that stung hard as BBs if you knew how
to put a spin on them. Ducking behind
gutted-out combines 'n coils of chicken wire,
we counted each scrape 'n scab testament
to grit, tough shit, truth, or consequence— scraped up
seed potatoes with sticks 'n fingernails
fooling ourselves they were gold enough
to buy our way out of town. As night tucked in,
our harvest turned to dirt-clod wars:
a little spit and dirt

                    could make some mud
                    could hide a stone
                    could hide a bruise

our skin
welted but unbroken—

When Asked Where I'm (Really) From

"To be Asian in America is to be quizzed, constantly, about your ethnicity. What are you? Where are you from? No, but where are your parents from?"

—Jeff Guo, *The Washington Post*

Between two halves of a canyon's split lip whose namesake the streets sing— all that is holy after opening day of hunting season: Remington, Winchester, Pistol Drive. Full of sandstone, gunpowder. No-stoplight town always taking at least two kids each year, pulled under by river snag, huffing Krylon Gold, accident of gorge's curve or gunshot. If asked, I'll tell you where I was made: wanting nothing but escape, the only girl who knew how to play— called to accompany wherever there was need. High school musical auditions, weddings, and ladies' Christmas teas. I was the girl who could sight-read a melody but had trouble keeping time, whose door a mother'd come knocking on in the middle of the night, come asking for a song.

Naturalization

When I came to this country, I was reborn
with a pistol in my palm.
They called me a natural:
That bullseye, gorgeous!

With a pistol in my palm
the weight like a future son,
that bullseye gorgeous
like summer sunlight on stainless steel.

The weight like a future son
dreaming blood on my hands—
like summer sunlight on stainless steel,
bright like Christ.

Dreaming blood on my hands,
they called me. A natural,
right? Like Christ,
when I came to: this country I was, reborn.

So blonde

it's almost white, I insisted that August
I convinced my best friend my hair turned gold
in the sun. That summer I was fooling whoever'd listen,
had Brandy and Crystal and Jessie believing
I heard Hanged Nelly giggle from a bathroom stall
and swore I was my mother's natural born daughter,
just came out looking like this, *a genetic anomaly.*
Most of them believed me for a minute or longer,
and sometimes I almost did, too— imagined a lilting
headful of tousled blonde, light as my baby brother's.
Pale enough the public pool tinted it green. Mine,
thick and black, so coarse when trimmed, the ends
splintered our bare feet. An unruly animal my mother
brushed daily— detangled and laced into days
of pigtails and braids, made me a pretty second
to the chestnut blonde Mormon twins
in French and Dutch plaits, headband halos,
and fishtails— before I refused to brush my hair
and conjured myself *a rat's nest*, but O how I loved
my horde of snarled darlings, so dark, so generous
of fur and tail and teeth.

Sonnet in Cold Blood

High June: the colder-blooded among us
are seeking shelter. The rat snake coils
behind the radiator, harmless. We still
don't risk proximity. Neighbors say *Kill*,
otherwise he will return, having learned
the way in. The first time, I was surprised—
expecting his blood somehow to be blue,
cold as I believed his kind to be.
But there it was on the pavement, as red
as mine. The next time I did it, his blood
was no less red but I was less
surprised. Reader, I want to tell you this
ends differently; I want to tell you the snake
was only a snake.

Prayer to Saint Martha

Late August the galley blooms
       fruit flies, smoke-winged and garnet-eyed, circling
the over-sweet caves

of pear and blueberry, clingstone
                      peach. Each night I pray resurrection

              but am deceived. Faith is not feast
but desire, not beauty of the table but what drags us starving there—

              what was buried inside
the sweetness— pearl-bright larvae within

the plum's rotten core. Saint dear
       of my difficult hunger:

              cloy me
                      mote me

       rise me up

Water Street Elegy

O Potomac   O dirty   O constant
     reviser. How sky forgets, scours even

our eulogies back to water, back
    to muck, to dirt. Flotsam, whiskey flask, and waterbird

lilt alike on river's filthy curl.
     Bones quiet under elms' ignorant shimmer.

June nods yes. Summer
    keeps on walking.

   Anemochory: balloon,   wing,   plume:
        the world loves still

to give, despite itself, its grief.

FALL

Equinox

The house begins to crawl
           with wasps budding
     from the ponderosa walls.

          The intruders
patrol our sills, creep
         through bed sheets,

sting us in sleep. They lord over
          the sandbox birch;
     their colonies hover from our eaves.

          At dusk, Father douses
their branch with gasoline.
          We strike the nest down

with sticks, tear through the coil, delicate
          as pastry in our fingers.
     In their folds: evidence

          of our lives: wisps of garden
mud, pulp filched
         from pine beams,

wound through the inner whorl
         of paper, a strand
     from the house's darkest head, mine.

Self-Portrait as Secret-Heart-of-Gold Boy

Never forget your anger, baby, a man once said to me, *that's where your power lies.* And I mistook this recognition for love, having always wanted to hold the two of them in the same hand— anger and power— like the boys in the movies I didn't know if I wanted or wanted to be. Bust-lipped, chip-shouldered boys: Jimmys, Tylers, Keiths, and Codys. Blue jean, black leather, always white. Guitar-riffed and bass-driven, crowd-parting boys swaggering into auto shop, locker room, guts of a flickering mall. Secret-Heart-of-Gold boys starving for their chance at glory— anointed Son, Bud, Untapped Potential, cooling off on the sidelines after a ref's bad call. Not the Good Girl I was, back of the ladies' choir bus, bubblegum-glossed and glittering like a scream. How I prayed to wake up believed in. Deserving. Swinging fists the maverick teacher calms just before the credits— *I see you.* And having been seen, therefore transfigured: boy turned endless field turned stadium at sunset, a burning multitude of men believing their empire will never stop winning.

Invasive Species

Something terrible happened today, I say
and my husband rushes to me, searching
for signs of harm. I do not want to tell him
the rest: how I found a tree frog in the door well
of our car, gazing up with what I then imagined
was hope, how I coaxed him into a paper sack
that I carried to a tree with plenty of shade
at the lot's far end, nudged the bag gently,
and waited. How when I returned,
he stared up at me, his leg now askew
from where I had broken it in my hurry.
His gaze was still the same, full not
with hope as I had once imagined but
something else. *I was just trying to help,* I say.
I knew that did not matter.

Aubade with Septic Field

The morning you leave, the white swamp oak chokes
    the septic lines, filling the tub and sinks with shit.

The plumber shows me this on his small camera:
    the gunky tunnel throat-like, slick with slime

and almost fleshly, sinker roots strangling
    the central pipe. A tree's roots, he says, can reach

as wide as its crown but it's impossible to tell
    from the surface. All summer the tree bloomed

three yards from our door, brushing our eaves
    with her catkins. And just beyond: the septic field

a dying stretch of grass behind the shed, a grave
    unmarked for our spoil. The day before you left,

the tree woke us, shrieking with grackles. If only
    we'd asked the birds, they would have told us

this does not happen overnight— each day we cave
    a little more, eave by lichen, pipe by crown,

giving ourselves over to what's entangled
    us long underground.

Hallasan

Jeju-do, South Korea

Stone flung to crater: we gather what we can of the dead, but they remember us in our entirety, filling our pockets with bones and pink rhododendron.

We pass the pavilion, toward the wooden skiff, its nets suspended in mud. You winnow through the ruin of the porous shore, your hands murky with sea urchins, palms stung with their dying stars. The basalt gods gaze on, graved full of moon. They eclipse dark at dusk. They are not our gods.

You move among them, absence constellating the fractured lights.

Animal Medicine

The pit bull's been pacing for days, gazing out
the screen door at ghost rabbits in the pasture,
circling around again, whimpering. He can't
understand the cost of finally belonging

to someone, of healing from so many years of neglect.
Three injections of melarsomine in three months,
deep in the hip, and we're only on the first round.
It's heartworms, so the alternative is agony:

larvae then a white skein of parasites threading
the arteries of the lungs before the heart
finally fails. Years ago in Tallahassee, I stood
in the black box theater, watching you direct

rehearsals for *This Property is Condemned*. I never saw you
so gentle. Pacing upstage, downstage. Begin at the end
and run all the way through. Unremarkable to watch
at first, then how the boy and girl began to soften,

each gesture yielding response, a sort of living-in.
I watched as they became Alva, became Owen—
but it was never about us. The beautiful sister was always
going to die. The worms will be gone by spring.

Aubade Before Storm

Beaufort, N.C.

The momentary calm having contained all that was and was
going to be, gust in breeze, swell tide-buried beyond the outer banks—

in the fescue, innocent as it appeared— the darkening

turn. Had we not been warned? We imagine voices calling to us, light
from the fishing boats, tiding fair weather

and believe no harm. The sun addressed us through the window—
quiet, solemn child— I tried to name you— memory is not a keeping

but a forgiving, the thresh and burn
of what we cannot salvage— and song is merely silence which

pierces some relentless
resonance: never is a sky

more beautiful than when ready to surrender its fury.

Did no one tell us? We cannot hold
        the drenched volume   of our world—

Field Dressing

I'd grown accustomed to circling the carcasses
already skinned, hanging neck-down in the garage
to tender the flesh, but I never understood how it began

until that Thanksgiving my father shot a doe
in our front yard. I ran up the hill to where
she had fled, watched the boys field dress her

in the clearing. How easily the muscle released
from the bone with a few, clean strokes: a deep
slit up the belly to peel back the hide, careful

not to taint the meat with the bladder's wet luster,
then up into the hollow between the neck and chest
to remove the trachea. A few taps from the hatchet

to separate the rib cage and expose the vitals. I caressed
the organs nestled together, gray-pink and smooth
as newborns. The boys divided the meat; one claimed

the pelt, another the hooves. The youngest boy
gave me the heart. I held the warm, fist-sized gem
until it cooled, then cast it to the dogs.

WINTER

How to Stay Warm

Night of the first frost, the furnace goes out.
I flip switches, elicit a few grunts.
Like anything, it goes until it can't.
Last of the oil gone, the orange float
bobbles bright at the gauge's empty line.
Again, the combustion chamber dies.
I'm here still, alone among the bare
magnolias, trying to remember
how to stay warm without a man.
I haul the space heater back from the barn
to the center of the room, watch it turn
my gray satellite to its tinseled sun.
In the middle of the night, a fuse blows:
as I sleep, the house descends again to cold.

Still Life with Fallen Game

At the edge of want,
       everything cast
              into ebbed relief; each

waxed and gorgeous object,
          but the distance between:

boar-shadow and bloodied quail,
       the negative space
                that is desire:

between what we want and what we are capable of,
          after-world:
overripe peach as slow eclipse ::: lover

                   turning afield,
hunger and fear, both brutal devotions

to what
       this dark bounty

       would hollow us into

Agency

I never cared much for their beauty, but admired how easily
the stallions could kill me. My aunt was thrown off a horse
at sixteen. She survived but never looked the same. All traces
of the family profile in the cheekbones and chin, gone.
Now, stumbling from dream and into the field, fists full
of peppermints, I plead to the animals, invisible over the hill
in the moonless night. I should know by now: it is never
about one's skill for finding, but the looked-for's willingness
to be found, just as a runaway girl is discovered only a block away
eating dinner at the neighbors' and no further, so her father
convinces himself that's all the little girl was capable of,
not what she wanted.
                          But tonight, the horses, there,
down among the beeches, know when I begin to yield
and do not move until I do, turning their heads
in the direction of my voice. Before I hear anything,
I feel it: their steeled hooves battering the frozen mud,
the valley itself trembling as they rush not toward,
but somehow beyond me, halting only
when they are close enough to pull me under.

Confession

I always liked Sundays best after a swallow
                of pear vodka from the thrift store stein,

        a chalice for all the gloomy boys

                                I was always seeing/not
seeing   I drank / he drank / I drank / he drank / we
        drank   that much closer   after each

                        cold gulp to holy.

Never really believed I'd find salvation
                in the valley of a man   but the saccharine haze
                        made me forget

                        what I tried to destroy—

        the stick figure christs   my childhood scrawled
in all my secret places—   I can confess now
        what I wanted

                        from those gloomy boys,
                                from that frosted glass,

                        was what I had once asked of God:
not to forget but to hover   outside myself

        just far enough to surrender   to being held

the last time I did this, enter
                a church buzzed, I mean,
                                was twenty paces after a cheap shot
        from a Brooklyn dive   after years without

anything sweet   just a couple widows and me,
a stranger

breathing sugar   under the chapel nave vaulting blue
                                        into a fizz of stars.

The World Just Now, Emerging

after the storm and the stillness that came before,
        we make our way down to the river,

past the autumn burn pile and the first stirrings
        of the birds in the apple tree.

My husband untangles himself from his winter woolens
        and lopes ahead, having known too much

of paradise to resist cold's threat,
        his back a fevered kite

tearing down the pale field:
        for each of his steps,

two of my own, heavy
        through the crisp lip of snow

as if a haul from some deep well,
        and I wonder if it will always be this way—

him forging ahead as I lose sight in the gray tangle
        of creeper and paper birch,

calling his name as if he were miles
        away and not a few paces,

reckless in my panic
        as I thrash through the brush,

afraid he will not wait,
        afraid I will leave him, waiting.

On the Feast of Epiphany

Tonight, the valley in lunar glow,
>the maples' darkboned host fishes visions

from ice. There is no marker but an invisible line
>dividing night from night, snow from snow.

There are no directions to the closest lighthouse, no signpost
>to tell how far from shore. As children here,

our mothers coaxed our tongues into prayers
>for mild winters and taught us to cull from them deliverance:

deer strung cruciform from shed rafters, cold blood cherries
>filling the cellar. We learned to play dead, knotting our hands

behind our necks to protect from grizzlies, to chisel
>breath-space in avalanche and trail the North Star home.

Tonight, my brother studies clouds, tells me
>the storm will break next morning. Once, I too could divine

first snow, but tonight, the heavens refuse me. The firmament
>rolls over, dreaming of other prophets.

Maryland Route 210, Dusk

It's the third or fourth
body this week. You've lost

count. Hard to tell from afar, first
mistaken for shredded tire

or garbage fallen from trucks
that only today, a week after

the blizzard, are running again.
You've come to learn

the shape of them, the way they lie
along the shoulder of the highway,

curled legs to abdomen, as if just borne
into the world. The body tonight

is not a man, though from fifty yards
it could have been, front legs thrown

around his head as if to shield
himself from a blow.

Tonight, this body does not belong
to a man but to a dog—

soft and well-cared for, the kind
that has a name written

on the collar you'd find
if you'd just pull over.

You don't.

Dead already, you reason.
Besides, it's dangerous to stop

even for a moment
in these dark and rushing hours—

no one would stop for you,
or the shape of you, inseparable

from the body you'd hover over
as headlights swept past you,

filing toward well-lit homes.

Elegy for Pyro

We constructed grief   in our image:
burning piano and Bud Light empties
sunk frozen in the field, mythed
your bones into a thing holdable
despite the godwant
of our hands

how to settle with absence
you / not you
you / winter landscape
you / oil rigs skeletal
in the night of you

they say funerals are for the living :::

but there is no one living here

the worst was after the wake
walking the pasture alone:

no longer the question
of what to say to night
once the dark too has forsaken
                what then

must we say to the inevitable sun
and to the day

stumbling after

and after,
that

SPRING

Parousia

Abandoned long enough, and a place becomes an elsewhere:
purple knapweed wilding the arches of the sunken
church, stone angels haloed in tillandsia, where
sometime between our leaving and return,
magpies perched and shat
until something grew.

Field Elegy

We carry the fawn down to the woods,
the body still light and lifelike, as if

it still carries some of the spirit, this animal
which only hours before had been crying

for its mother, abandoned in an open field.
I sit with the fawn as my husband digs and digs,

striking roots and rocks until he finds a soft place
where the soil has some give. I can't stop

touching the small pink wound in its spotted side
— or the belly, still soft beneath a ribcage

a smidge bigger than my fist. I fold the slender legs
neatly as if bedding it down, and lower the body

into the hole (I say lower, though the hole
is only shin-deep, just enough to keep the dogs

from dragging the carcass back to the house).
I flinch as the body topples over, its hooves tangling

in oak roots. Even though I know the suffering is over,
I want to shut its round black eye, now dulling

as it stares up through the soil— I want to make it
look as if it were sleeping and not dead

— as if such a thing were a mercy
to this fawn and not to me, now alone

in this field and bleating.

After Easter

Of course, the flowers were dead
to begin with, cut as they were,
but three days after Easter,
they've begun to rot, and Pastor Mark
jokes the church smells like a funeral.
Why shouldn't it? Christ may have risen,
but nothing lasts forever.
I walk the sanctuary, pull stems
from murky vases, brush petals
from the choir loft. This year,
the lilies, named after dead
saints or the *glory of God*, refused
to open, despite trying to force
their blooms with hairdryers.
Back home, Easter had everyone
in our town driving the twilit hours
to the houses of the dying for sunrise
service, the early hours clawing up
our throats as we sang *Up From the Grave
He Arose* into the bluing hills. I'd run
into the weeds, gorge on fistfuls
of sugar birds, and dare our dead Christ
to rise from my green body.

Aubade at Low Tide

We walked for miles on the sand's firm ribs, afterthoughts
        of high tide strung among them: sea glass, ghost shrimp,

lion's mane jellyfish. Finally married: my mother's relief
        and the rings to prove it, carved with waves

from some ancient obelisk. This after the six months
        my neurons were cut cables in a dark tunnel—

I shrugged myself on again,   nerves cool and wet
        under my dress. Mornings

I took the train across the Mersey River to wander
        the ruins of churches smoldering purple

with loosestrife and storm, the cathedral aglow
        with pink script: *I felt you and I knew you loved me.*

I waited for him to return, my arms full
        of takeout cartons blistered with rain,

a few perfect apples; those afternoons I believed the rest
        of our lives could be this damp, green and free, before

my wires began arcing live again
        beneath my nightgown sleeves—

Nocturne with Seven Isles

I.

From here, I climb the narrow island
through moon rock, shallows wide and white
as desert and survivor-littered:
jellyfish cruel and translucent in sea grass,
starfish drying beneath armor,
sand dollars melting black velvet.

Even the sea cannot contain itself:

I reel in a small sunfish, gill-torn,
but still I toss him back,
as if by returning alone—
as if salvation—

only the limp float of his bright underside
a thin slice of flame among the reeds.

I taste the salt on my lips,
wonder if this is how it began
for the woman who turned
against God to watch her only city burn.

II.

We unearth places we once lived, the house
        sundered by lichen, drawers withering
    with summer herbs, the mammal
                    scent of soured boots,
        cedar fronds rotting
                rooftop gutters. Tell me
about the brass bed frame,
        what love once wracked there
                and of its leaving. Tell me
of each fountain swan, feathers greened with sea
        air. Sing me the names of everything lost,
    each ash and wing. Invent them if you must.

III.

I listen everywhere for the psalm
that echoed off the stone walls
in the winter chapel:
yet is their strength labor and sorrow;
       for it is soon cut off, and we fly away.
Ives' dissonant harmonies like walls shuddering
inward— we spend our days as a tale that is told—

sacrament, sacrilege alike an edge
against which we hollow
ourselves—

I sand the music as if the melody
could sculpt our sinews back to bone.

IV.

Months tide shores of unanswered letters;
I write you as if you were dead.

I think of collapse, its Latin roots
meaning to fall together— imagine

cathedral arches, spine-sharp
                    leaning to imprison
saints radiant in shards—

now, too late, I understand
            I did not mistake desire
but its direction— somewhere beyond—
            a music half-remembering itself.

Look how we fail in increments
like last century's estates, opening
into stone arches;
                    even as we refuse
to go, see how the body takes us there, without
            our blessing or consent.

V.

afterward,   you exhaled   quiet for once
possibly content   for an hour we breathed
late light there   two solitudes   pooled together
then   unlike time and time before   I just turned

the brass knob and watched you leave   our rucksack history
slung over your shoulder   in that silence   we discovered
the door   we'd razed cities and sabotaged bridges to   find

VI.

I excavate a lamp
from the basement—
how satisfying to draw
the shade taut, to tear
bulb from carton and pull
the chain. To make light.
        I need to see
                what I agreed
                to leave;

is it the light
I love or is it leaving
everything else in darkness?

The empty room asks:
Now, then, what do you want?

VII.

Here, tangerines like paper lanterns
wait for night to rob their glow.
Oil on the canal as if from a dreamer,
beneath. Here, let us claw
match and flint; let us ask with fire
what the water has forgotten.

Epithalamium with Spider and Sparrow

See what our bodies make
of each other, my seraph sung
from reed and seeding stalks;
my blue-mouthed beauty—
see what ellipses we
spin and snare, radiant
limb and muddied wing.

.

Perennis Amor

Walking together,
        you speak the names

you've learned passing through:
        iris,   ranunculus,

calla lily,   plum—
        recount how the garden is

always changing: lilacs fragrant
        first, then the cascade

of wisteria, and now
        high summer's roses.

May love be that
        which endures, transforming

with its endurance:
        foxglove's quiet

between biennial songs,
        the helleborus' burst

in snow, the lean
        of sunflowers toward the sun.

May love be all that weights
        and awaits each,

all that is green within the sapling,
        seed, and loam.

Nocturne with Volcanoes and Honey

Tonight, this sweetness has no recollection
        of the garden, no memory of those

two million hive-to-flower journeys
        its laborers require for even one

pound of honey. It is forgetting the irises and cosmos,
        dirt and root, finds impossible to trace

the quadrille of drone in wax catacomb,
        refuses to name each pollen spore and sepal,

weightless with solitude:
        this teaspoon of a countless world

stirred and dissolved— the having been and lost.
        Each year, fifty to seventy volcanoes erupt

around the world, not only the St. Helens and Pompeiis
        but also the nameless and submerged,

earth upheaved and churning itself anonymous
        crescents, then islands, then atlases of blooms.

Tell me what happens
after paradise: when everything

we could have wished for
has been given, but we're still here;

what to do with having
survived, which is to say,

trudging no longer through
the briars of what-could-have-been,

but scavenging fallows after hail:
orchard of after,

grieved but mercy-wild
look how it is glinting   now   sunlight
now icelight   now   green

kindling what lasted
at last in us.

Notes

"Matthew 19:14" owes a great debt to Jericho Brown, whose model of re-envisioning Biblical scripture in his collection *The New Testament* paved the way for this poem and others in this collection. *The New Testament* provided a model and a path for me to follow in exploring, interrogating, and re-imagining the scriptures that I was brought up with during my own childhood and which still continue to haunt me.

The epigraph for "Where I'm (Really) From" comes from an article, "Every Asian American has been asked this question. A computer gives the best answer," by Jeff Guo that appeared in *The Washington Post* on October 21, 2016 about scientists at the University of Rochester who attempted to teach an algorithm that distinguished between the faces of Chinese, Korean, and Japanese people.

"Water Street Elegy" is dedicated to V.C.

"Animal Medicine" takes its title from a scene from Tennessee Williams's *This Property is Condemned* in which Willie falls on the railroad tracks and injures herself, and her friend Tom tells her, "Spit on it. That takes the sting away. [...] That's animal medicine, you know. They always lick their wounds."

"Elegy for Pyro" is dedicated to Capt. William "Pyro" DuBois.

"Aubade at Low Tide"— the words in italics are taken from Tracey Emin's "For You" installation, which can be seen in the Liverpool Cathedral.

The italicized text in section IV of "Nocturne with Seven Isles" refers to the King James Version of Psalm 90 and to the musical composition titled after the psalm by the American composer Charles Ives.

"Perennis Amor" is dedicated to C.A. and M.C. and takes its title from an inscription on a statue by Harriet W. Frishmuth entitled, "Roses of Yesterday" in the Brooklyn Botanic Garden.

Thank You

Thank you to my editor, Marci Calabretta Cancio-Bello, Erin Elizabeth Smith, and the rest of the Sundress Publications family for their care and attention throughout the process of bringing *Arabilis* into the world. Love and gratitude to Margaret Bashaar for nominating my manuscript for the Sundress open reading period and for being one of the first to advocate for my work as an emerging poet.

My deepest love and gratitude to those people and communities who have walked alongside me as these poems made, and sometimes clawed, their way into the world: to Kundiman (and especially my mentor Jennifer Chang), VONA, Jericho Brown's workshop at Tin House Summer Workshop, Laure-Anne Bosselaar's workshop at the U.S. Poets in Mexico retreat, to the folks at the MFA program at the University of Miami, including M. Evelina Galang, Mia Leonin, John Murillo, and Maureen Seaton—and to Lee Herrick, who supported me from afar.

Thanks to my friends and literary family who lent loving support to me and critical insight to these poems, without which this collection would not exist: Kate Debolt, Rachel Gray, Luke Hankins, Phil Lacey, Tiana Nobile, Ansley Moon, Hannah Oberman-Breindel, Essy Stone, and Kent Szlauderbach. I remain grateful to Mr. E and Mr. W. and the Waterford family for their enduring support for my work. Love and the utmost gratitude always to Justin Engles and to my family: David, Mary, Kyle, Evan, Mariah (and the boys), Mike, Ingrid, Kevin, Rachael, and to Sean, who has always been the sunlight in all of my seasons.

About the Author

Leah Silvieus is the author of *Arabilis* (Sundress Publications), *Anemochory* (Hyacinth Girl Press) and *Season of Dares* (Bull City Press). She holds a B.A. from Whitworth University and an M.F.A. from the University of Miami. She is a Kundiman Fellow and currently serves as Books Editor at *Hyphen* magazine.

Other Sundress Titles

Afakasi | Half-Caste
Hali F. Sofala-Jones
$16

Marvels
MR Sheffield
$20

Match Cut
Letitia Trent
$16

Passing Through Humansville
Karen Craigo
$16

Divining Bones
Charlie Bondus
$16

Phantom Tongue
Steven Sanchez
$15

Citizens of the Mausoleum
Rodney Gomez
$15

The Minor Territories
Danielle Sellers
$15

Either Way, You're Done
Stephanie McCarley Dugger
$15

Actual Miles
Jim Warner
$15

Hands That Break and Scar
Sarah A. Chavez
$15

Before Isadore
Shannon Elizabeth Hardwick
$15

They Were Bears
Sarah Marcus
$15

Big Thicket Blues
Natalie Giarratano
$15

Babbage's Dream
Neil Aitken
$15

At Whatever Front
Les Kay
$15

Posada
Xochitl Julisa Bermejo
$15

Suites for the Modern Dancer
Jill Khoury
$15

www.ingramcontent.com/pod-product-compliance
Lightning Source LLC
Chambersburg PA
CBHW031149090426
42738CB00008B/1274